Vivian Yuen

JENNY
AND GRANDPA

What is it like to be old?

By Carolyn Nystrom
Illustrated by Shirley Bellwood

A LION BOOK
Tring • Batavia • Sydney

For Lori and both her Grandpas

Text copyright © 1988 Carolyn Nystrom
This illustrated edition © 1988 Lion Publishing

Published by
Lion Publishing Corporation
1705 Hubbard Avenue, Batavia, Illinois 60510, USA
ISBN 0 7459 1396 2

First edition 1988

Library of Congress Cataloging-in-Publication Data

Nystrom, Carolyn.
  Jenny and Grandpa: what is it like to be old?
  by Carolyn Nystrom: illustrated by Shirley Bellwood—
  1st ed.
  p.   cm.
  "A Lion book."
  ISBN 0–7459–1396–2
  [1. Grandfathers—Fiction.   2. Old age—Fiction.
  3. Death—Fiction.]   I. Large, Annabel, ill.   II. Title.
  PZ7.N996Jac 1987   87-15643

Printed and bound in Belgium

    "Grandpa, what's it like to be old?" Jenny asked, as
she braced her sixty pounds against the long wooden
plank her grandfather held firm with one hand across
his battered sawhorse.
    "Old?" Grandpa drew a straight line with his blunt-
shaved carpenter's pencil, then set his saw in place.
"I'm not old. I'm seventy five years young."

Grandpa was like that.

Just now he was making over her closet with shelves and drawers and cubbyholes, and rods at different heights for dresses, pants, and skirts. Jenny had seen an ad for a remodeled closet in a children's magazine.

"You'd like a closet like that, Sweet Patoodie?" Grandpa had asked. "I'll be over on Tuesday."

Grandpa hadn't always built closet shelves. Just a few years ago, Grandpa was building houses—some of the biggest and best houses in Brookville. Jenny could

remember visiting Grandpa at work then. She'd seen him walk tall along the high beams of a second floor with a heavy load of lumber balanced on his shoulder. She'd seen him drive four-inch nails into planks with three rhythmic swings of his hammer. She'd seen him creep along a newly laid wood floor on his hands and knees while he sanded them smooth as woven silk.

    But Grandpa didn't build houses anymore. Grandpa
was retired. Sure, he wore the same carpenter's
overalls and carried the same tool box and bent over
the same sawhorse and drove the same battered truck.
But Grandpa didn't build houses. He built closet
shelves and rehung doors and repaired broken chairs.
And sometimes he just sat on his front porch and
waited for people to stop by and talk. Jenny stopped by
a lot.

A person who retires is an older person who stops working at his or her regular job. Some companies require that employees stop working at a certain age, like sixty five or seventy. People like Jenny's Grandpa who don't work for a company may decide for their own reasons that they no longer want to work all day every day. Perhaps they don't feel as well or as strong as they used to. Maybe they want to take time to be with friends or to travel. Or maybe they just want more time to rest.

Often people who retire choose to do exciting things they have waited for all of their lives. They may learn to sail a boat, photograph wild animals in Africa, or spend a winter in Alaska.

"Ouch," Grandpa grunted.

Jenny felt alarm as she glimpsed a thin trickle of red on his right forefinger. "What's wrong? Are you hurt?" she asked.

"Nothing major," Grandpa replied. "I guess I just picked up this board wrong." He examined a small cut. "It's time we cleaned up for today anyway. We can finish the job tomorrow."

Jenny found a bandaid in the bathroom medicine cabinet, then helped Grandpa clean and cover his cut. It seemed a little funny putting a bandaid on Grandpa. Last time they had raided the first aid supply, it was Grandpa patching up her elbow after a roller skating spill. But today, Grandpa didn't seem to mind a little help.

Bandage job completed, they swept up sawdust together, then stacked the waiting lumber out of the way against the wall. (Grandpa was always strict about not leaving a mess, even if he were coming back to the same job the next day.)

"Would you like a little lesson in electric drill work tomorrow, my friend?" Grandpa asked.

Jenny felt a rush of anticipation as she nodded. Grandpa had always promised to teach her to use his power tools, but the time had always been "someday". It appeared that someday had finally come.

Jenny hugged her knees tight under her chin as they
rattled down Main Street in Grandpa's high truck cab.
The truck seat felt sun-baked hot. She squinted against
the glare of heat ripples above the pavement. Even the
broad maple leaves hung limp as if to conserve some
remaining moisture. Grandpa rested his arm on the
open truck window, ignoring the heat, and shaded his
eyes as he wheeled into the dusty parking lot of Dari
Freeze.

Minutes later they were settled in the relative cool
of Grandpa's front porch, licking at the last drips of
ice cream. Jenny always ate straight down from the

top, but Grandpa kept pushing his down with his tongue so that there was ice cream all the way to the bottom. Grandpa said he felt disappointed if he got to the last bite and there was nothing left but empty shell.

"Bong, bong, bong," shouted the town clock—three o'clock. Mom would be home from her office job at the feed mill in another hour and a half. Then Jenny would walk the short block to her own house. During the summer, Jenny kept Grandpa company while Mom worked.

15

"What's it like to be old, Grandpa?" Jenny asked again.

Grandpa sent her a quizzical look.

"Really," she persisted.

"Well, when you are old you remember a lot," Grandpa said slowly.

"What do you remember, Grandpa?" Jenny asked as she settled comfortably against the porch post.

Grandpa thought a minute. "I remember my senior year of high school right here in Brookville." Grandpa

grunted and settled back on the porch bench.

Jenny thought his eyes looked like they were seeing something far away.

"I'd been out of school for awhile. Times were hard then, and my family was always short of money for food. I'd go to school for a year or so, then stay home and work the farm so that we could get a little food ahead, then I'd come back to school for a year. By the time I finally got to the end, I was twenty five years old."

"Why did you keep coming back?" Jenny asked.

"I'm not sure," Grandpa said thoughtfully. "I was the youngest in my family and nobody else had gone to school any more than three or four years. But I really liked to learn. I guess I just decided to be different."

"Did you and Grandma go on dates?" Jenny giggled.

"Depends on what you call dates, I guess," Grandpa replied. "We didn't have money and I didn't have a car. But on weekends, I'd walk out to the farm where she lived."

"How far?" Jenny asked.

"Oh, about ten miles, I guess. Used to take me almost three hours."

Jenny gasped.

"But your Grandma would be waiting for me, all dressed up so pretty it was worth every footstep. Then we'd sit in the parlor and talk, with her mom or dad peeping in every few minutes. About ten o'clock her dad would come in and wind the big clock on the mantle. Then I knew I'd better leave, or else."

"Did you walk all the way back the same night?" Jenny asked.

"Sometimes," Grandpa sighed. "But other times," he chuckled, "I'd just walk another couple miles up the road and stay with my aunt, so I could come back the next day."

"When did you get married?" Jenny asked.

"A year or so later," Grandpa said. "We finished school, graduated together. We both worked that summer and saved money."

"Did you have a big wedding?"

"Not hardly," Grandpa laughed. "Our little country church only held about forty people. We were married one Sunday morning after services. We each had a friend stand up with us, said our vows to the pastor and people, then we ran out of the church and had a picnic with everyone."

Grandpa looked down at his left hand, gnarled hard by fifty years of carpentry but still supporting a gold band, worn thin.

"I miss your Grandma so much," he said with trembly voice.

"I know," Jenny said. She rested her head against his arm. "I wish I had known her."

People who are old often feel lonely—even with lots of people around. When they were young, they made good friends, and they kept being friends throughout the important events of their lives: marriage, children, jobs. Going through these changes together helped them to love each other even more.

But as people get older something hard begins to happen. The people they love most begin to die. Perhaps the first big loss is a parent, then both parents. Soon some friends their own age die. Then the hardest loss comes: a wife or husband dies. After a while, it seems that no one close to them is left. So they feel alone.

Children can help older people by understanding why they are lonely. They can listen to stories about people from their past. Most older people are glad to have a new young friend.

Next day, Jenny and her Grandpa squatted in her open closet. Grandpa held his power drill in one hand as he explained the array of bits.

"You use this bit for big holes like drilling into cement for expanding bolts," he said, picking up a bit the size of her thumb. "But this one," he shifted to one the size of a pencil, "is just right for hinge screws." Then he moved to a slender bit at the end. "This is the one we'll use today."

Grandpa showed her how to fit the bit into the drill, then how to brace its weight so she wouldn't get hurt. But then he laid the drill aside and got out his tape measure. "Measure twice, drill once," he said, as he measured and marked throughout her closet. Then he went through the entire closet and measured every

spot again. No mistakes. By the end of the day, Jenny
was measuring, marking—and drilling.

Jenny rubbed her arm muscles as she rode in the
truck cab the short distance to Grandpa's house. She
could still feel the powerful quiver of the drill in her
hand. It was a good kind of tired.

Suddenly the truck gave a clunking grinding roar
and shuddered to a stop. Blue smoke seeped from
under the hood. Grandpa climbed out to take a closer
look.

Later that evening, Grandpa unloaded all the tools from his truck. Jenny helped him carry them home and stack them on the porch. Then they watched a tow truck hoist the front of Grandpa's truck high and haul it to Riley's Repair. Jenny wondered how Grandpa's sturdy truck could suddenly look so frail and helpless.

Next day, Jenny was up early. She knew Grandpa would be awake too. Grandpa always got up at five o'clock to read his Bible and pray before the day started. There was no reason to get up so early now that he was retired. He could just as easily sleep until eight or nine and still have time to read and pray. But, of his early morning hours, Grandpa just said, "Old habits die hard."

Jenny said a quiet prayer of her own. She thanked God for her family, and for her new closet under construction, and for the sky already tinged blue—the same shade as chicory.

By eight o'clock, she was feeling cool dew on her toes through the straps of her sandals as she scampered to Grandpa's. She found Grandpa on the phone with a serious expression on his face.

"How much?"

"One thousand dollars? But the truck is hardly
worth that much!"

"I understand."

"I'll let you know this afternoon."

"Thank you, too. Goodbye."

Grandpa replaced the phone and held his arm out to
Jenny for a good morning hug.

"Bad news on the truck, Grandpa?" Jenny asked.

"I'm afraid so. It looks like I'll have to junk it."

"But how will you get around? You'll buy another truck, won't you?"

"I don't think so," Grandpa replied. "That would cost a lot more money than I can spend now."

"Oh, Grandpa, I liked your truck so much," Jenny said, as she leaned against his chest. "It's hard to believe we'll never ride in it again."

"I know, Sweet Patoodie." Grandpa stroked her
hair. "I've seen a lot of good times in that truck, even
before you were born." His eyes looked far away.

"I'm afraid part of being old," Grandpa continued,
"is giving up some things—especially things that cost a
lot of money."

Jenny sighed.

That day, they walked to Jenny's house—and carried
tools all the way.

Many old people are not able to buy the things they could when they were younger. They may have worked hard and saved money, as Jenny's Grandpa did, but once they stop working, they no longer earn new money. The money they spend may come from money they saved, or money from a company retirement fund, or money from the government, but it will certainly not be as much as they had while they were working. Besides that, prices may be much higher than when they were younger and saved the money. Even worse, they may have extra expenses, like high medical costs.

To cope with these problems, many older people move to smaller houses or apartments. They may sell their car, or just not replace an old one. They may buy fewer new clothes. They learn to be careful about using too much heat or light. They may choose to eat less expensive foods.

Children can help older people by being thankful for small gifts from them. That may seem hard, if grandparents once gave costly gifts like bicycles and stereos, and now they give a book or a pair of gloves. But the small gift comes with just as much love as the big one. More important, children can learn to value gifts from older people that cost no money at all. Jenny's Grandfather is giving her a gift worth much more than money. He is teaching her building skills that took him a lifetime to learn.

Three days later, Grandpa and Jenny stood arm in
arm admiring the results of their week's work. They
had measured and sawed and drilled and hammered
and sanded and painted. Each day Jenny had done a
little more of the work. She wasn't ready yet to start
fitting out closets on her own, but she knew a lot
about them. Hammer, saw, drill, and paint brush all
felt at home in her hand. And the result was
fantastic—even better than she had dreamed. She
could hardly wait to move all of her things into it.
That new closet was like having an extra room.

One last job remained: clean-up. Grandpa always
insisted on leaving a work site better than he had
found it, and the hottest day of summer didn't change
his standards one bit. Jenny felt sweat drip off her nose
and onto her dust cloth as she cleaned sawdust from
furniture tops. Her tee shirt clung wet to her back.
Grandpa knelt on hands and knees, head buried in the
closet, to sweep the last bit of wood shavings from the
corners. He emerged red-faced with his pile of debris
and started to stand. Suddenly, he fell over on his side,
rolled onto his back, and lay still.

"Grandpa!" Jenny shouted.

Grandpa just groaned softly.

Jenny ran to him, heart pounding, and shook him gently. "Grandpa?"

Still no answer. Grandpa was breathing fast, but he didn't move and he didn't talk.

Jenny rushed to the phone. Her hand shook so much she could hardly dial. Somehow she managed to reach 911, ask for an ambulance, and give her address. Then

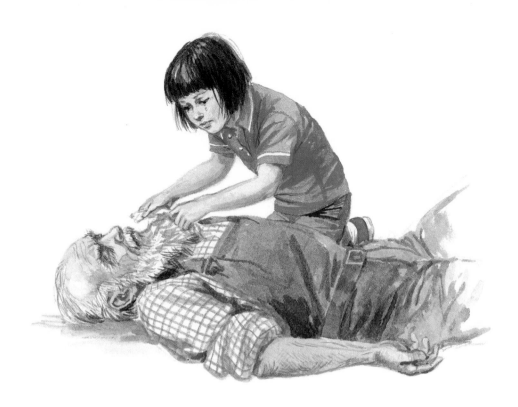

she called her mother at work.

She ran back to Grandpa. He was still breathing fast but he hadn't moved. He felt hot, so she wet a towel with cold water and began to wash his face. She felt the familiar scratch of gray beard against her hand. Would Grandpa ever hug her against that beard again?

An ambulance siren screamed in the distance. Jenny felt a sob clutch at her throat.

Two paramedics clattered into the room with heavy equipment cases. They listened to Grandpa's heart, took his temperature and blood pressure, then put a needle in Grandpa's arm to give him extra fluid. They spoke kindly to Jenny, but they were busy with Grandpa. Still, Grandpa did not wake up. Jenny sat cross-legged on her bed and cried softly.

A few minutes later, she stood in the doorway and watched the paramedics wheel Grandpa to the ambulance. She reached out and touched Grandpa's hand as he passed. For a moment, he opened his eyes and looked at her. Jenny thought she saw a faint smile.

"God, please take care of him," she whispered as the ambulance disappeared down the street.

Just then, her mother wheeled into the driveway and held open the car door.

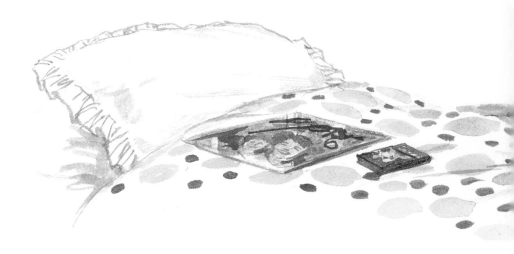

Moments later, they were at the hospital.

From the emergency room doorway, Jenny could barely see her Grandfather strapped to a high bed surrounded by white uniformed people.

"Wait here," her mother said, and walked straight in. Jenny saw her touch Grandpa, then turn toward the medical workers.

"Heart . . . stroke . . . heat . . ." and lots of words she didn't understand drifted toward her.

Jenny tried to tell her Mom about finishing the closet, but that didn't seem important anymore. She tried to look at magazines, but couldn't think about what was in front of her. She walked around the waiting room and looked out the window, but couldn't see anything but Grandpa lying on her bedroom floor.

Soon her mother returned with a nurse to fill out medical forms: age, date of birth, past illnesses, insurance.

Then they waited. And waited.

Finally, a white-coated doctor stepped toward them. "Would you like to see him?"

"Is he . . . ?" her mother began.

"He's going to be fine," the doctor smiled. "We wondered for a bit. There is so much to consider in a person his age. But I think he just got too much heat."

Jenny felt a one ton weight drop from her shoulders.

"We'd like to keep him in the hospital for a couple of days," the doctor went on. "But I think by the end of the week you'll see him back much better."

One of the most discouraging parts of being old is changes in the body: wrinkles, gray hair, dry skin—sometimes with brown spots. Some older people worry that these changes make them look ugly. Yet photographers use old people as models for some of their most beautiful pictures.

Other body changes are not as easy to see. An older person's bones break more easily—and it takes longer for them to heal. Cuts and scratches take longer to heal too. Muscles begin to wear out; they are not as strong, and they tire more easily.

Arthritis, a disease that causes sore swollen joints, makes it hard to walk, lift, or do hard work. Eyes and ears may not work as well as they once did, so it's harder to see and hear. Even going to the bathroom is hard. Muscles inside the body aren't as strong as they used to be, so older people may have bathroom accidents, just as a young child does.

The hardest body changes are in the brain. A few older people have trouble remembering.

Sometimes older people have so many body changes that they can no longer care for themselves. Then their adult children take care of the parent, just as the old person once took care of them.

These body changes in an older person may frighten children who love them—just as Jenny was frightened to see her Grandfather so ill. But children can help in many ways. Just remember that older people are still grown-ups, grown-ups who need a little extra care.

Jenny stood next to Grandpa's hospital bed. Gray chest hair bristled above his hospital gown. Clear fluid still dripped through a needle in his arm. His breathing was slow and even. He looked asleep.

"Grandpa?" she whispered.

Grandpa opened his eyes. "Hey, Sweet Patoodie." He reached out an arm.

Jenny buried her face on his chest. "Oh, Grandpa. Are you really alright?"

"They tell me I'm going to be fine." He stroked her hair. "Next time though, I'm supposed to act my age— be a little more careful about mixing work and heat."

"I was so scared," Jenny whispered.

"I know," Grandpa said. "But say," he held her shoulders so he could look her straight in the face, "scared or not, you did a great job taking care of me. Thanks."

A week later, Jenny sat across the table from
Grandpa in his sunny kitchen. A cool breeze blew his
yellow checked curtain inward and fanned Jenny's hair
away from her face. Grandpa's Bible still lay open to
the book of Isaiah, where he had been reading that
morning. Grandpa looked a little pale, and Jenny
noticed that his right hand shook as he poured coffee
from his battered coffee pot.

"Grandpa?" Jenny asked. "What if I hadn't been
with you when you got sick? What if . . . ?"

Grandpa stopped her. "No what if's," he said. "You
were there and so was God. Even if you had not been
there, God is always with me."

"But you might have died!"

"That's true," Grandpa answered. "But dying is not so terrible."

Jenny shuddered. She wasn't sure she agreed.

"Let me show you what God said to Isaiah," Grandpa went on. "I read chapter 46 just this morning."

I have cared for you from the
*   time you were born.*
I am your God and will take
*   care of you*
until you are old and your
*   hair is gray.*
I made you and will care for you . . .

Grandpa stopped reading. "God has always taken care of me—and he will keep on taking care of me. Someday God will take care of me by taking me to heaven to be with him."

Grandpa pushed his chair away. "But not just yet. Right now I have no truck, but I have two good feet." He stood briskly, then swayed a little and leaned forward, hands braced against the table.

"It's just that the legs aren't so steady," he said with a thin smile.

Jenny smiled back, but her forehead creased a worry wrinkle.

"I think I can still walk though," Grandpa said, "if my favorite walking partner doesn't mind a little slower pace."

Jenny stood too. "I saw some chicory growing right near the path," she said.

Moments later they plodded through the field behind Grandpa's house. They stopped to admire a fern, to watch a bee buzz from blossom to blossom, to listen to a small animal scuttering unseen through the grasses. Sometimes they stopped for no reason at all— so Grandpa could rest.

Jenny led the way while Grandpa rested his hand on her shoulder. She felt the tremble of his hand enter her own body, then stop solid as if braced against her own small young strength.

"Grandpa?" Jenny asked. "Will I get old?"

"Most likely," he answered.

They were silent for a moment—thinking.

Then Jenny spoke again. "Grandpa, when I'm old, I hope I'm just like you."

"And when you are old," Grandpa added, "I hope God gives you a special young friend, too."